CW00693323

Copyright © 2020 by Judion Smith

FIRST EDITION

ISBN: 9798642148181

Imprint: Independently Published

www.nurturingtheextraordinary.com

Hearts of Gratitude

FAMILY JOURNAL

Judion Smith

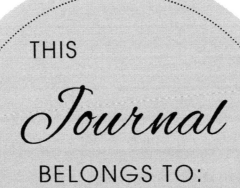

THIS

Journal

BELONGS TO:

Attitude of Gratitude

Gratitude is awareness and appreciation towards someone or something of value that makes a profound impact on our life. Gratitude widens our frame of vision in a way that changes our perceptions on life, moving us from "I want," towards "I have," and into a place of "I appreciate." The expression of gratitude comes when we truly realize the importance of others, as we acknowledge the fundamental part they play in our lives.

Gratitude gives much attention to the small victories that are sometimes ignored or overlooked, as we become transfixed on the supposedly bigger things that would have caused the massive breakthrough that we think we need. Gratitude keeps us from always wanting more, to see the more that is already in what we have. The prison of always wanting more will rob us of our health. As we put immense stress on our minds, it ends up reflecting on our health. It is very much the norm to look around and desire more, but never at the extent of losing our physical or mental health. Our appetite as human beings is sometimes immensely influenced by society's expectations of us, as we are driven by materialist consumption to prove our worth. We become stressed and depressed, trying to fit in and losing our peace and sense of gratitude along the way. Our desire for more has caused us to unconsciously ignore the people and things that matter the most. Having a desire is not the real issue that we are faced with, but rather it is not being appreciative of what we have and becoming sick and depressed because of what we don't have.

Gratitude prevents us from becoming consumed by what we should have and lets us appreciate the fact that we have all we need. We should be grateful that every-thing we need we already have, and all that we desire is additional luxury that we can live without. Our health is our wealth. Let us not lose it at the expense of be-ing overwhelmed or consumed by the desire for more. Let us use our present mo-ment to be grateful for what we are indeed blessed with, and when the crav-ings for more come upon us, let us remind ourselves that we have all that we need. It is through our widened lens of gratitude that we realize that less is indeed more.

would like to share with you some of the core benefits of gratitude. These include, but are by no means limited to:

Spiritual Growth - Acknowledgment of our own inability to sustain ourselves will point us straight to the source by which we are sustained. Our attitude of gratitude towards our creator will create a connection and a dependency on Him to supply all that we need. We will understand the part He plays in our lives.

Those who matter to us will know – Too often, we fail to express to our loved ones what they truly mean to us and how grateful we are for their presence in our lives. Too often, we lose them to the grave and find ourselves speaking over their dead bodies how much they meant to us. Sometimes, it is knowing how much they mean to us and how much we appreciate them that will assist them on their journey through life.

Healthier Minds – Gratitude will birth joy and peace in our soul, keeping our minds free from strong holds. It takes our mind to a healthier place of positivity, as we delight in the people and things that we are indeed blessed with. Stress, depression, and anxiety are the result of us wanting and craving for more, without taking the time to appreciate what we do have. In the midst of chasing things, we can easily lose sight of what matters most. Overwhelming thoughts of desires will make us sick, while thoughts of gratitude create an atmosphere of appreciation that satisfies our soul.

Positive Mindset – Gratitude takes us away from negative feelings to positive ones. We counteract negative emotions as we make a conscious decision to see the positives in our lives. Grateful people are more positive and healthier. They are in a more positive state of being than those who fail to see the good in their life experiences.

A New Attitude – Being grateful is a habit worth having. It is time we create habits that work for us. The way we think, feel, and act towards things will determine how we move forward and the kinds of doors that will open for us.

A Radiant Glow – Hearts that are full of gratitude glow differently. They give off a radiant glow, as they are free from being overwhelmed with distress. Hearts that are full of gratitude maintain their positive state of being and are more able to retain peace and contentment.

How To Use This Journal

This journal is to record the things and people that you are grateful for. It can be used for daily or weekly recordings, whether at the beginning or the end of the day. Everyone who makes a recording will sign their name. The family can choose to have a discussion as to why they are grateful for the things or people they recorded.

I Am Grateful

Today, I am grateful for

Name:

Date:

Today, I am grateful for

Name:

Date:

Today, I am grateful for

Name:

Date:

Today, I am grateful for

Name:

Date:

I Am Grateful

Today, I am grateful for

Name:

Date:

Today, I am grateful for

Name:

Date:

Today, I am grateful for

Name:

Date:

Today, I am grateful for

Name:

Date:

I Am Grateful

Today, I am grateful for

Name:

Date:

Today, I am grateful for

Name:

Date:

Today, I am grateful for

Name:

Date:

Today, I am grateful for

Name:

Date:

I Am Grateful

Today, I am grateful for

Name:

Date:

Today, I am grateful for

Name:

Date:

Today, I am grateful for

Name:

Date:

Today, I am grateful for

Name:

Date:

I Am Grateful

Today, I am grateful for

Name:

Date:

Today, I am grateful for

Name:

Date:

Today, I am grateful for

Name:

Date:

Today, I am grateful for

Name:

Date:

I Am Grateful

Today, I am grateful for

Name:

Date:

Today, I am grateful for

Name:

Date:

Today, I am grateful for

Name:

Date:

Today, I am grateful for

Name:

Date:

I Am Grateful

Today, I am grateful for

Name:

Date:

Today, I am grateful for

Name:

Date:

Today, I am grateful for

Name:

Date:

Today, I am grateful for

Name:

Date:

I Am Grateful

Today, I am grateful for

Name:

Date:

Today, I am grateful for

Name:

Date:

Today, I am grateful for

Name:

Date:

Today, I am grateful for

Name:

Date:

I Am Grateful

Today, I am grateful for

Name:

Date:

Today, I am grateful for

Name:

Date:

Today, I am grateful for

Name:

Date:

Today, I am grateful for

Name:

Date:

I Am Grateful

Today, I am grateful for

Name:

Date:

Today, I am grateful for

Name:

Date:

Today, I am grateful for

Name:

Date:

Today, I am grateful for

Name:

Date:

I Am Grateful

Today, I am grateful for

Name:

Date:

Today, I am grateful for

Name:

Date:

Today, I am grateful for

Name:

Date:

Today, I am grateful for

Name:

Date:

I Am Grateful

Today, I am grateful for

Name:

Date:

Today, I am grateful for

Name:

Date:

Today, I am grateful for

Name:

Date:

Today, I am grateful for

Name:

Date:

I Am Grateful

Today, I am grateful for

Name:

Date:

Today, I am grateful for

Name:

Date:

Today, I am grateful for

Name:

Date:

Today, I am grateful for

Name:

Date:

I Am Grateful

Today, I am grateful for

Name:

Date:

Today, I am grateful for

Name:

Date:

Today, I am grateful for

Name:

Date:

Today, I am grateful for

Name:

Date:

I Am Grateful

Today, I am grateful for

Name:

Date:

Today, I am grateful for

Name:

Date:

Today, I am grateful for

Name:

Date:

Today, I am grateful for

Name:

Date:

I Am Grateful

Today, I am grateful for

Name:

Date:

Today, I am grateful for

Name:

Date:

Today, I am grateful for

Name:

Date:

Today, I am grateful for

Name:

Date:

I Am Grateful

Today, I am grateful for

Name:

Date:

Today, I am grateful for

Name:

Date:

Today, I am grateful for

Name:

Date:

Today, I am grateful for

Name:

Date:

I Am Grateful

Today, I am grateful for

Name:

Date:

Today, I am grateful for

Name:

Date:

Today, I am grateful for

Name:

Date:

Today, I am grateful for

Name:

Date:

I Am Grateful

Today, I am grateful for

Name:

Date:

Today, I am grateful for

Name:

Date:

Today, I am grateful for

Name:

Date:

Today, I am grateful for

Name:

Date:

I Am Grateful

Today, I am grateful for

Name:

Date:

Today, I am grateful for

Name:

Date:

Today, I am grateful for

Name:

Date:

Today, I am grateful for

Name:

Date:

I Am Grateful

Today, I am grateful for

Name:

Date:

Today, I am grateful for

Name:

Date:

Today, I am grateful for

Name:

Date:

Today, I am grateful for

Name:

Date:

I Am Grateful

Today, I am grateful for

Name:

Date:

Today, I am grateful for

Name:

Date:

Today, I am grateful for

Name:

Date:

Today, I am grateful for

Name:

Date:

I Am Grateful

Today, I am grateful for

Name:

Date:

Today, I am grateful for

Name:

Date:

Today, I am grateful for

Name:

Date:

Today, I am grateful for

Namc:

Date:

I Am Grateful

Today, I am grateful for

Name:

Date:

Today, I am grateful for

Name:

Date:

Today, I am grateful for

Name:

Date:

Today, I am grateful for

Name:

Date:

I Am Grateful

Today, I am grateful for

Name:

Date:

Today, I am grateful for

Name:

Date:

Today, I am grateful for

Name:

Date:

Today, I am grateful for

Name:

Date:

I Am Grateful

Today, I am grateful for

Name:

Date:

Today, I am grateful for

Name:

Date:

Today, I am grateful for

Name:

Date:

Today, I am grateful for

Name:

Date:

I Am Grateful

Today, I am grateful for

Name:

Date:

Today, I am grateful for

Name:

Date:

Today, I am grateful for

Name:

Date:

Today, I am grateful for

Name:

Date:

I Am Grateful

Today, I am grateful for

Name:

Date:

Today, I am grateful for

Name:

Date:

Today, I am grateful for

Name:

Date:

Today, I am grateful for

Name:

Date:

I Am Grateful

Today, I am grateful for

Name:

Date:

Today, I am grateful for

Name:

Date:

Today, I am grateful for

Name:

Date:

Today, I am grateful for

Name:

Date:

I Am Grateful

Today, I am grateful for

Name:

Date:

Today, I am grateful for

Name:

Date:

Today, I am grateful for

Name:

Date:

Today, I am grateful for

Name:

Date:

I Am Grateful

Today, I am grateful for

Name:

Date:

Today, I am grateful for

Name:

Date:

Today, I am grateful for

Name:

Date:

Today, I am grateful for

Name:

Date:

I Am Grateful

Today, I am grateful for

Name:

Date:

Today, I am grateful for

Name:

Date:

Today, I am grateful for

Name:

Date:

Today, I am grateful for

Name:

Date:

I Am Grateful

Today, I am grateful for

Name:

Date:

Today, I am grateful for

Name:

Date:

Today, I am grateful for

Name:

Date:

Today, I am grateful for

Name:

Date:

I Am Grateful

Today, I am grateful for

Name:

Date:

Today, I am grateful for

Name:

Date:

Today, I am grateful for

Name:

Date:

Today, I am grateful for

Name:

Date:

I Am Grateful

Today, I am grateful for

Name:

Date:

Today, I am grateful for

Name:

Date:

Today, I am grateful for

Name:

Date:

Today, I am grateful for

Name:

Date:

Today, I am grateful for

Name:

Date:

Today, I am grateful for

Name:

Date:

Today, I am grateful for

Name:

Date:

Today, I am grateful for

Name:

Date:

I Am Grateful

Today, I am grateful for

Name:

Date:

Today, I am grateful for

Name:

Date:

Today, I am grateful for

Name:

Date:

Today, I am grateful for

Name:

Date:

Today, I am grateful for

Name:

Date:

Today, I am grateful for

Name:

Date:

Today, I am grateful for

Name:

Date:

Today, I am grateful for

Name:

Date:

I Am Grateful

Today, I am grateful for

Name:

Date:

Today, I am grateful for

Name:

Date:

Today, I am grateful for

Name:

Date:

Today, I am grateful for

Name:

Date:

I Am Grateful

Today, I am grateful for

Name:

Date:

Today, I am grateful for

Name:

Date:

Today, I am grateful for

Name:

Date:

Today, I am grateful for

Name:

Date:

I Am Grateful

Today, I am grateful for

Name:

Date:

Today, I am grateful for

Name:

Date:

Today, I am grateful for

Name:

Date:

Today, I am grateful for

Name:

Date:

I Am Grateful

Today, I am grateful for

Name:

Date:

Today, I am grateful for

Name:

Date:

Today, I am grateful for

Name:

Date:

Today, I am grateful for

Name:

Date:

I Am Grateful

Today, I am grateful for

Name:

Date:

Today, I am grateful for

Name:

Date:

Today, I am grateful for

Name:

Date:

Today, I am grateful for

Name:

Date:

Today, I am grateful for

Name:

Date:

Today, I am grateful for

Name:

Date:

Today, I am grateful for

Name:

Date:

Today, I am grateful for

Name:

Date:

I Am Grateful

Today, I am grateful for

Name:

Date:

Today, I am grateful for

Name:

Date:

Today, I am grateful for

Name:

Date:

Today, I am grateful for

Name:

Date:

I Am Grateful

Today, I am grateful for

Name:

Date:

Today, I am grateful for

Name:

Date:

Today, I am grateful for

Name:

Date:

Today, I am grateful for

Name:

Date:

I Am Grateful

Today, I am grateful for

Name:

Date:

Today, I am grateful for

Name:

Date:

Today, I am grateful for

Name:

Date:

Today, I am grateful for

Name:

Date:

I Am Grateful

Today, I am grateful for

Name:

Date:

Today, I am grateful for

Name:

Date:

Today, I am grateful for

Name:

Date:

Today, I am grateful for

Name:

Date:

I Am Grateful

Today, I am grateful for

Name:

Date:

Today, I am grateful for

Name:

Date:

Today, I am grateful for

Name:

Date:

Today, I am grateful for

Name:

Date:

I Am Grateful

Today, I am grateful for

Name:

Date:

Today, I am grateful for

Name:

Date:

Today, I am grateful for

Name:

Date:

Today, I am grateful for

Name:

Date:

I Am Grateful

Today, I am grateful for

Name:

Date:

Today, I am grateful for

Name:

Date:

Today, I am grateful for

Name:

Date:

Today, I am grateful for

Name:

Date:

I Am Grateful

Today, I am grateful for

Name:

Date:

Today, I am grateful for

Name:

Date:

Today, I am grateful for

Name:

Date:

Today, I am grateful for

Name:

Date:

I Am Grateful

Today, I am grateful for

Name:

Date:

Today, I am grateful for

Name:

Date:

Today, I am grateful for

Name:

Date:

Today, I am grateful for

Name:

Date:

I Am Grateful

Today, I am grateful for

Name:

Date:

Today, I am grateful for

Name:

Date:

Today, I am grateful for

Name:

Date:

Today, I am grateful for

Name:

Date:

I Am Grateful

Today, I am grateful for

Name:

Date:

Today, I am grateful for

Name:

Date:

Today, I am grateful for

Name:

Date:

Today, I am grateful for

Name:

Date:

I Am Grateful

Today, I am grateful for

Name:

Date:

Today, I am grateful for

Name:

Date:

Today, I am grateful for

Name:

Date:

Today, I am grateful for

Name:

Date:

I Am Grateful

Today, I am grateful for

Name:

Date:

Today, I am grateful for

Name:

Date:

Today, I am grateful for

Name:

Date:

Today, I am grateful for

Name:

Date:

Today, I am grateful for

Name:

Date:

Today, I am grateful for

Name:

Date:

Today, I am grateful for

Name:

Date:

Today, I am grateful for

Name:

Date:

I Am Grateful

Today, I am grateful for

Name:

Date:

Today, I am grateful for

Name:

Date:

Today, I am grateful for

Name:

Date:

Today, I am grateful for

Name:

Date:

I Am Grateful

Today, I am grateful for

Name:

Date:

Today, I am grateful for

Name:

Date:

Today, I am grateful for

Name:

Date:

Today, I am grateful for

Name:

Date:

I Am Grateful

Today, I am grateful for

Name:

Date:

Today, I am grateful for

Name:

Date:

Today, I am grateful for

Name:

Date:

Today, I am grateful for

Name:

Date:

I Am Grateful

Today, I am grateful for

Name:

Date:

Today, I am grateful for

Name:

Date:

Today, I am grateful for

Name:

Date:

Today, I am grateful for

Name:

Date:

I Am Grateful

Today, I am grateful for

Name:

Date:

Today, I am grateful for

Name:

Date:

Today, I am grateful for

Name:

Date:

Today, I am grateful for

Name:

Date:

I Am Grateful

Today, I am grateful for

Name:

Date:

Today, I am grateful for

Name:

Date:

Today, I am grateful for

Name:

Date:

Today, I am grateful for

Name:

Date:

I Am Grateful

Today, I am grateful for

Name:

Date:

Today, I am grateful for

Name:

Date:

Today, I am grateful for

Name:

Date:

Today, I am grateful for

Name:

Date:

I Am Grateful

Today, I am grateful for

Name:

Date:

Today, I am grateful for

Name:

Date:

Today, I am grateful for

Name:

Date:

Today, I am grateful for

Name:

Date:

I Am Grateful

Today, I am grateful for

Name:

Date:

Today, I am grateful for

Name:

Date:

Today, I am grateful for

Name:

Date:

Today, I am grateful for

Name:

Date:

Today, I am grateful for

Name:

Date:

Today, I am grateful for

Name:

Date:

Today, I am grateful for

Name:

Date:

Today, I am grateful for

Name:

Date:

I Am Grateful

Today, I am grateful for

Name:

Date:

Today, I am grateful for

Name:

Date:

Today, I am grateful for

Name:

Date:

Today, I am grateful for

Name:

Date:

I Am Grateful

Today, I am grateful for

Name:

Date:

Today, I am grateful for

Name:

Date:

Today, I am grateful for

Name:

Date:

Today, I am grateful for

Name:

Date:

I Am Grateful

Today, I am grateful for

Name:

Date:

Today, I am grateful for

Name:

Date:

Today, I am grateful for

Name:

Date:

Today, I am grateful for

Name:

Date:

I Am Grateful

Today, I am grateful for

Name:

Date:

Today, I am grateful for

Name:

Date:

Today, I am grateful for

Name:

Date:

Today, I am grateful for

Name:

Date:

I Am Grateful

Today, I am grateful for

Name:

Date:

Today, I am grateful for

Name:

Date:

Today, I am grateful for

Name:

Date:

Today, I am grateful for

Name:

Date:

I Am Grateful

Today, I am grateful for

Name:

Date:

Today, I am grateful for

Name:

Date:

Today, I am grateful for

Name:

Date:

Today, I am grateful for

Name:

Date:

I Am Grateful

Today, I am grateful for

Name:

Date:

Today, I am grateful for

Name:

Date:

Today, I am grateful for

Name:

Date:

Today, I am grateful for

Name:

Date:

I Am Grateful

Today, I am grateful for

Name:

Date:

Today, I am grateful for

Name:

Date:

Today, I am grateful for

Name:

Date:

Today, I am grateful for

Name:

Date:

I Am Grateful

Today, I am grateful for

Name:

Date:

Today, I am grateful for

Name:

Date:

Today, I am grateful for

Name:

Date:

Today, I am grateful for

Name:

Date:

I Am Grateful

Today, I am grateful for

Name:

Date:

Today, I am grateful for

Name:

Date:

Today, I am grateful for

Name:

Date:

Today, I am grateful for

Name:

Date:

I Am Grateful

Today, I am grateful for

Name:

Date:

Today, I am grateful for

Name:

Date:

Today, I am grateful for

Name:

Date:

Today, I am grateful for

Name:

Date:

I Am Grateful

Today, I am grateful for

Name:

Date:

Today, I am grateful for

Name:

Date:

Today, I am grateful for

Name:

Date:

Today, I am grateful for

Name:

Date:

I Am Grateful

Today, I am grateful for

Name:

Date:

Today, I am grateful for

Name:

Date:

Today, I am grateful for

Name:

Date:

Today, I am grateful for

Name:

Date:

I Am Grateful

Today, I am grateful for

Name:

Date:

Today, I am grateful for

Name:

Date:

Today, I am grateful for

Name:

Date:

Today, I am grateful for

Name:

Date:

I Am Grateful

Today, I am grateful for

Name:

Date:

Today, I am grateful for

Name:

Date:

Today, I am grateful for

Name:

Date:

Today, I am grateful for

Name:

Date:

I Am Grateful

Today, I am grateful for

Name:

Date:

Today, I am grateful for

Name:

Date:

Today, I am grateful for

Name:

Date:

Today, I am grateful for

Name:

Date:

Today, I am grateful for

Name:

Date:

Today, I am grateful for

Name:

Date:

Today, I am grateful for

Name:

Date:

Today, I am grateful for

Name:

Date:

I Am Grateful

Today, I am grateful for

Name:

Date:

Today, I am grateful for

Name:

Date:

Today, I am grateful for

Name:

Date:

Today, I am grateful for

Name:

Date:

I Am Grateful

Today, I am grateful for

Name:

Date:

Today, I am grateful for

Name:

Date:

Today, I am grateful for

Name:

Date:

Today, I am grateful for

Name:

Date:

I Am Grateful

Today, I am grateful for

Name:

Date:

Today, I am grateful for

Name:

Date:

Today, I am grateful for

Name:

Date:

Today, I am grateful for

Name:

Date:

I Am Grateful

Today, I am grateful for

Name:

Date:

Today, I am grateful for

Name:

Date:

Today, I am grateful for

Name:

Date:

Today, I am grateful for

Name:

Date:

I Am Grateful

Today, I am grateful for

Name:

Date:

Today, I am grateful for

Name:

Date:

Today, I am grateful for

Name:

Date:

Today, I am grateful for

Name:

Date:

I Am Grateful

Today, I am grateful for

Name:

Date:

Today, I am grateful for

Name:

Date:

Today, I am grateful for

Name:

Date:

Today, I am grateful for

Name:

Date:

I Am Grateful

Today, I am grateful for

Name:

Date:

Today, I am grateful for

Name:

Date:

Today, I am grateful for

Name:

Date:

Today, I am grateful for

Name:

Date:

I Am Grateful

Today, I am grateful for

Name:

Date:

Today, I am grateful for

Name:

Date:

Today, I am grateful for

Name:

Date:

Today, I am grateful for

Name:

Date:

I Am Grateful

Today, I am grateful for

Name:

Date:

Today, I am grateful for

Name:

Date:

Today, I am grateful for

Name:

Date:

Today, I am grateful for

Name:

Date:

I Am Grateful

Today, I am grateful for

Name:

Date:

Today, I am grateful for

Name:

Date:

Today, I am grateful for

Name:

Date:

Today, I am grateful for

Name:

Date:

I Am Grateful

Today, I am grateful for

Name:

Date:

Today, I am grateful for

Name:

Date:

Today, I am grateful for

Name:

Date:

Today, I am grateful for

Name:

Date:

I Am Grateful

Today, I am grateful for

Name:

Date:

Today, I am grateful for

Name:

Date:

Today, I am grateful for

Name:

Date:

Today, I am grateful for

Name:

Date:

I Am Grateful

Today, I am grateful for

Name:

Date:

Today, I am grateful for

Name:

Date:

Today, I am grateful for

Name:

Date:

Today, I am grateful for

Name:

Date:

I Am Grateful

Today, I am grateful for

Name:

Date:

Today, I am grateful for

Name:

Date:

Today, I am grateful for

Name:

Date:

Today, I am grateful for

Name:

Date:

I Am Grateful

Today, I am grateful for

Name:

Date:

Today, I am grateful for

Name:

Date:

Today, I am grateful for

Name:

Date:

Today, I am grateful for

Name:

Date:

I Am Grateful

Today, I am grateful for

Name:

Date:

Today, I am grateful for

Name:

Date:

Today, I am grateful for

Name:

Date:

Today, I am grateful for

Name:

Date:

I Am Grateful

Today, I am grateful for

Name:

Date:

Today, I am grateful for

Name:

Date:

Today, I am grateful for

Name:

Date:

Today, I am grateful for

Name:

Date:

I Am Grateful

Today, I am grateful for

Name:

Date:

Today, I am grateful for

Name:

Date:

Today, I am grateful for

Name:

Date:

Today, I am grateful for

Name:

Date:

I Am Grateful

Today, I am grateful for

Name:

Date:

Today, I am grateful for

Name:

Date:

Today, I am grateful for

Name:

Date:

Today, I am grateful for

Name:

Date:

I Am Grateful

Today, I am grateful for

Name:

Date:

Today, I am grateful for

Name:

Date:

Today, I am grateful for

Name:

Date:

Today, I am grateful for

Name:

Date:

I Am Grateful

Today, I am grateful for

Name:

Date:

Today, I am grateful for

Name:

Date:

Today, I am grateful for

Name:

Date:

Today, I am grateful for

Name:

Date:

I Am Grateful

Today, I am grateful for

Name:

Date:

Today, I am grateful for

Name:

Date:

Today, I am grateful for

Name:

Date:

Today, I am grateful for

Name:

Date:

I Am Grateful

Today, I am grateful for

Name:

Date:

Today, I am grateful for

Name:

Date:

Today, I am grateful for

Name:

Date:

Today, I am grateful for

Name:

Date:

I Am Grateful

Today, I am grateful for

Name:

Date:

Today, I am grateful for

Name:

Date:

Today, I am grateful for

Name:

Date:

Today, I am grateful for

Name:

Date:

I Am Grateful

Today, I am grateful for

Name:

Date:

Today, I am grateful for

Name:

Date:

Today, I am grateful for

Name:

Date:

Today, I am grateful for

Name:

Date:

I Am Grateful

Today, I am grateful for

Name:

Date:

Today, I am grateful for

Name:

Date:

Today, I am grateful for

Name:

Date:

Today, I am grateful for

Name:

Date:

I Am Grateful

Today, I am grateful for

Name:

Date:

Today, I am grateful for

Name:

Date:

Today, I am grateful for

Name:

Date:

Today, I am grateful for

Name:

Date:

I Am Grateful

Today, I am grateful for

Name:

Date:

Today, I am grateful for

Name:

Date:

Today, I am grateful for

Name:

Date:

Today, I am grateful for

Name:

Date:

I Am Grateful

Today, I am grateful for

Name:

Date:

Today, I am grateful for

Name:

Date:

Today, I am grateful for

Name:

Date:

Today, I am grateful for

Name:

Date:

I Am Grateful

Today, I am grateful for

Name:

Date:

Today, I am grateful for

Name:

Date:

Today, I am grateful for

Name:

Date:

Today, I am grateful for

Name:

Date:

I Am Grateful

Today, I am grateful for

Name:

Date:

Today, I am grateful for

Name:

Date:

Today, I am grateful for

Name:

Date:

Today, I am grateful for

Name:

Date:

I Am Grateful

Today, I am grateful for

Name:

Date:

Today, I am grateful for

Name:

Date:

Today, I am grateful for

Name:

Date:

Today, I am grateful for

Name:

Date:

I Am Grateful

Today, I am grateful for

Name:

Date:

Today, I am grateful for

Name:

Date:

Today, I am grateful for

Name:

Date:

Today, I am grateful for

Name:

Date:

I Am Grateful

Today, I am grateful for

Name:

Date:

Today, I am grateful for

Name:

Date:

Today, I am grateful for

Name:

Date:

Today, I am grateful for

Name:

Date:

I Am Grateful

Today, I am grateful for

Name:

Date:

Today, I am grateful for

Name:

Date:

Today, I am grateful for

Name:

Date:

Today, I am grateful for

Name:

Date:

I Am Grateful

Today, I am grateful for

Name:

Date:

Today, I am grateful for

Name:

Date:

Today, I am grateful for

Name:

Date:

Today, I am grateful for

Name:

Date:

I Am Grateful

Today, I am grateful for

Name:

Date:

Today, I am grateful for

Name:

Date:

Today, I am grateful for

Name:

Date:

Today, I am grateful for

Name:

Date:

I Am Grateful

Today, I am grateful for

Name:

Date:

Today, I am grateful for

Name:

Date:

Today, I am grateful for

Name:

Date:

Today, I am grateful for

Name:

Date:

I Am Grateful

Today, I am grateful for

Name:

Date:

Today, I am grateful for

Name:

Date:

Today, I am grateful for

Name:

Date:

Today, I am grateful for

Name:

Date:

I Am Grateful

Today, I am grateful for

Name:

Date:

Today, I am grateful for

Name:

Date:

Today, I am grateful for

Name:

Date:

Today, I am grateful for

Name:

Date:

I Am Grateful

Today, I am grateful for

Name:

Date:

Today, I am grateful for

Name:

Date:

Today, I am grateful for

Name:

Date:

Today, I am grateful for

Name:

Date:

I Am Grateful

Today, I am grateful for

Name:

Date:

Today, I am grateful for

Name:

Date:

Today, I am grateful for

Name:

Date:

Today, I am grateful for

Name:

Date:

I Am Grateful

Today, I am grateful for

Name:

Date:

Today, I am grateful for

Name:

Date:

Today, I am grateful for

Name:

Date:

Today, I am grateful for

Name:

Date:

I Am Grateful

Today, I am grateful for

Name:

Date:

Today, I am grateful for

Name:

Date:

Today, I am grateful for

Name:

Date:

Today, I am grateful for

Name:

Date:

I Am Grateful

Today, I am grateful for

Name:

Date:

Today, I am grateful for

Name:

Date:

Today, I am grateful for

Name:

Date:

Today, I am grateful for

Name:

Date:

I Am Grateful

Today, I am grateful for

Name:

Date:

Today, I am grateful for

Name:

Date:

Today, I am grateful for

Name:

Date:

Today, I am grateful for

Name:

Date:

I Am Grateful

Today, I am grateful for

Name:

Date:

Today, I am grateful for

Name:

Date:

Today, I am grateful for

Name:

Date:

Today, I am grateful for

Name:

Date:

I Am Grateful

Today, I am grateful for

Name:

Date:

Today, I am grateful for

Name:

Date:

Today, I am grateful for

Name:

Date:

Today, I am grateful for

Name:

Date:

I Am Grateful

Today, I am grateful for

Name:

Date:

Today, I am grateful for

Name:

Date:

Today, I am grateful for

Name:

Date:

Today, I am grateful for

Name:

Date:

I Am Grateful

Today, I am grateful for

Name:

Date:

Today, I am grateful for

Name:

Date:

Today, I am grateful for

Name:

Date:

Today, I am grateful for

Name:

Date:

I Am Grateful

Today, I am grateful for

Name:

Date:

Today, I am grateful for

Name:

Date:

Today, I am grateful for

Name:

Date:

Today, I am grateful for

Name:

Date:

I Am Grateful

Today, I am grateful for

Name:

Date:

Today, I am grateful for

Name:

Date:

Today, I am grateful for

Name:

Date:

Today, I am grateful for

Name:

Date:

I Am Grateful

Today, I am grateful for

Name:

Date:

Today, I am grateful for

Name:

Date:

Today, I am grateful for

Name:

Date:

Today, I am grateful for

Name:

Date:

I Am Grateful

Today, I am grateful for

Name:

Date:

Today, I am grateful for

Name:

Date:

Today, I am grateful for

Name:

Date:

Today, I am grateful for

Name:

Date:

I Am Grateful

Today, I am grateful for

Name:

Date:

Today, I am grateful for

Name:

Date:

Today, I am grateful for

Name:

Date:

Today, I am grateful for

Name:

Date:

I Am Grateful

Today, I am grateful for

Name:

Date:

Today, I am grateful for

Name:

Date:

Today, I am grateful for

Name:

Date:

Today, I am grateful for

Name:

Date:

Today, I am grateful for

Name:

Date:

Today, I am grateful for

Name:

Date:

Today, I am grateful for

Name:

Date:

Today, I am grateful for

Name:

Date:

I Am Grateful

Today, I am grateful for

Name:

Date:

Today, I am grateful for

Name:

Date:

Today, I am grateful for

Name:

Date:

Today, I am grateful for

Name:

Date:

I Am Grateful

Today, I am grateful for

Name:

Date:

Today, I am grateful for

Name:

Date:

Today, I am grateful for

Name:

Date:

Today, I am grateful for

Name:

Date:

I Am Grateful

Today, I am grateful for

Name:

Date:

Today, I am grateful for

Name:

Date:

Today, I am grateful for

Name:

Date:

Today, I am grateful for

Name:

Date:

I Am Grateful

Today, I am grateful for

Name:

Date:

Today, I am grateful for

Name:

Date:

Today, I am grateful for

Name:

Date:

Today, I am grateful for

Name:

Date:

I Am Grateful

Today, I am grateful for

Name:

Date:

Today, I am grateful for

Name:

Date:

Today, I am grateful for

Name:

Date:

Today, I am grateful for

Name:

Date:

I Am Grateful

Today, I am grateful for

Name:

Date:

Today, I am grateful for

Name:

Date:

Today, I am grateful for

Name:

Date:

Today, I am grateful for

Name:

Date:

I Am Grateful

Today, I am grateful for

Name:

Date:

Today, I am grateful for

Name:

Date:

Today, I am grateful for

Name:

Date:

Today, I am grateful for

Name:

Date:

I Am Grateful

Today, I am grateful for

Name:

Date:

Today, I am grateful for

Name:

Date:

Today, I am grateful for

Name:

Date:

Today, I am grateful for

Name:

Date:

I Am Grateful

Today, I am grateful for

Name:

Date:

Today, I am grateful for

Name:

Date:

Today, I am grateful for

Name:

Date:

Today, I am grateful for

Name:

Date:

I Am Grateful

Today, I am grateful for

Name:

Date:

Today, I am grateful for

Name:

Date:

Today, I am grateful for

Name:

Date:

Today, I am grateful for

Name:

Date:

I Am Grateful

Today, I am grateful for

Name:

Date:

Today, I am grateful for

Name:

Date:

Today, I am grateful for

Name:

Date:

Today, I am grateful for

Name:

Date:

Today, I am grateful for

Name:

Date:

Today, I am grateful for

Name:

Date:

Today, I am grateful for

Name:

Date:

Today, I am grateful for

Name:

Date:

I Am Grateful

Today, I am grateful for

Name:

Date:

Today, I am grateful for

Name:

Date:

Today, I am grateful for

Name:

Date:

Today, I am grateful for

Name:

Date:

I Am Grateful

Today, I am grateful for

Name:

Date:

Today, I am grateful for

Name:

Date:

Today, I am grateful for

Name:

Date:

Today, I am grateful for

Name:

Date:

I Am Grateful

Today, I am grateful for

Name:

Date:

Today, I am grateful for

Name:

Date:

Today, I am grateful for

Name:

Date:

Today, I am grateful for

Name:

Date:

I Am Grateful

Today, I am grateful for

Name:

Date:

Today, I am grateful for

Name:

Date:

Today, I am grateful for

Name:

Date:

Today, I am grateful for

Name:

Date:

I Am Grateful

Today, I am grateful for

Name:

Date:

Today, I am grateful for

Name:

Date:

Today, I am grateful for

Name:

Date:

Today, I am grateful for

Name:

Date:

I Am Grateful

Today, I am grateful for

Name:

Date:

Today, I am grateful for

Name:

Date:

Today, I am grateful for

Name:

Date:

Today, I am grateful for

Name:

Date:

I Am Grateful

Today, I am grateful for

Name:

Date:

Today, I am grateful for

Name:

Date:

Today, I am grateful for

Name:

Date:

Today, I am grateful for

Name:

Date:

Today, I am grateful for

Name:

Date:

Today, I am grateful for

Name:

Date:

Today, I am grateful for

Name:

Date:

Today, I am grateful for

Name:

Date:

I Am Grateful

Today, I am grateful for

Name:

Date:

Today, I am grateful for

Name:

Date:

Today, I am grateful for

Name:

Date:

Today, I am grateful for

Name:

Date:

Today, I am grateful for

Name:

Date:

Today, I am grateful for

Name:

Date:

Today, I am grateful for

Name:

Date:

Today, I am grateful for

Name:

Date:

I Am Grateful

Today, I am grateful for

Name:

Date:

Today, I am grateful for

Name:

Date:

Today, I am grateful for

Name:

Date:

Today, I am grateful for

Name:

Date:

I Am Grateful

Today, I am grateful for

Name:

Date:

Today, I am grateful for

Name:

Date:

Today, I am grateful for

Name:

Date:

Today, I am grateful for

Name:

Date:

I Am Grateful

Today, I am grateful for

Name:

Date:

Today, I am grateful for

Name:

Date:

Today, I am grateful for

Name:

Date:

Today, I am grateful for

Name:

Date:

I Am Grateful

Today, I am grateful for

Name:

Date:

Today, I am grateful for

Name:

Date:

Today, I am grateful for

Name:

Date:

Today, I am grateful for

Name:

Date:

I Am Grateful

Today, I am grateful for

Name:

Date:

Today, I am grateful for

Name:

Date:

Today, I am grateful for

Name:

Date:

Today, I am grateful for

Name:

Date:

I Am Grateful

Today, I am grateful for

Name:

Date:

Today, I am grateful for

Name:

Date:

Today, I am grateful for

Name:

Date:

Today, I am grateful for

Name:

Date:

I Am Grateful

Today, I am grateful for

Name:

Date:

Today, I am grateful for

Name:

Date:

Today, I am grateful for

Name:

Date:

Today, I am grateful for

Name:

Date:

I Am Grateful

Today, I am grateful for

Name:

Date:

Today, I am grateful for

Name:

Date:

Today, I am grateful for

Name:

Date:

Today, I am grateful for

Name:

Date:

I Am Grateful

Today, I am grateful for

Name:

Date:

Today, I am grateful for

Name:

Date:

Today, I am grateful for

Name:

Date:

Today, I am grateful for

Name:

Date:

I Am Grateful

Today, I am grateful for

Name:

Date:

Today, I am grateful for

Name:

Date:

Today, I am grateful for

Name:

Date:

Today, I am grateful for

Name:

Date:

I Am Grateful

Today, I am grateful for

Name:

Date:

Today, I am grateful for

Name:

Date:

Today, I am grateful for

Name:

Date:

Today, I am grateful for

Name:

Date:

I Am Grateful

Today, I am grateful for

Name:

Date:

Today, I am grateful for

Name:

Date:

Today, I am grateful for

Name:

Date:

Today, I am grateful for

Name:

Date:

I Am Grateful

Today, I am grateful for

Name:

Date:

Today, I am grateful for

Name:

Date:

Today, I am grateful for

Name:

Date:

Today, I am grateful for

Name:

Date:

I Am Grateful

Today, I am grateful for

Name:

Date:

Today, I am grateful for

Name:

Date:

Today, I am grateful for

Name:

Date:

Today, I am grateful for

Name:

Date:

I Am Grateful

Today, I am grateful for

Name:

Date:

Today, I am grateful for

Name:

Date:

Today, I am grateful for

Name:

Date:

Today, I am grateful for

Name:

Date:

I Am Grateful

Today, I am grateful for

Name:

Date:

Today, I am grateful for

Name:

Date:

Today, I am grateful for

Name:

Date:

Today, I am grateful for

Name:

Date:

I Am Grateful

Today, I am grateful for

Name:

Date:

Today, I am grateful for

Name:

Date:

Today, I am grateful for

Name:

Date:

Today, I am grateful for

Name:

Date:

I Am Grateful

Today, I am grateful for

Name:

Date:

Today, I am grateful for

Name:

Date:

Today, I am grateful for

Name:

Date:

Today, I am grateful for

Name:

Date:

I Am Grateful

Today, I am grateful for

Name:

Date:

Today, I am grateful for

Name:

Date:

Today, I am grateful for

Name:

Date:

Today, I am grateful for

Name:

Date:

I Am Grateful

Today, I am grateful for

Name:

Date:

Today, I am grateful for

Name:

Date:

Today, I am grateful for

Name:

Date:

Today, I am grateful for

Name:

Date:

I Am Grateful

Today, I am grateful for

Name:

Date:

Today, I am grateful for

Name:

Date:

Today, I am grateful for

Name:

Date:

Today, I am grateful for

Name:

Date:

I Am Grateful

Today, I am grateful for

Name:

Date:

Today, I am grateful for

Name:

Date:

Today, I am grateful for

Name:

Date:

Today, I am grateful for

Name:

Date:

I Am Grateful

Today, I am grateful for

Name:

Date:

Today, I am grateful for

Name:

Date:

Today, I am grateful for

Name:

Date:

Today, I am grateful for

Name:

Date:

I Am Grateful

Today, I am grateful for

Name:

Date:

Today, I am grateful for

Name:

Date:

Today, I am grateful for

Name:

Date:

Today, I am grateful for

Name:

Date:

I Am Grateful

Today, I am grateful for

Name:

Date:

Today, I am grateful for

Name:

Date:

Today, I am grateful for

Name:

Date:

Today, I am grateful for

Name:

Date:

I Am Grateful

Today, I am grateful for

Name:

Date:

Today, I am grateful for

Name:

Date:

Today, I am grateful for

Name:

Date:

Today, I am grateful for

Name:

Date:

I Am Grateful

Today, I am grateful for

Name:

Date:

Today, I am grateful for

Name:

Date:

Today, I am grateful for

Name:

Date:

Today, I am grateful for

Name:

Date:

I Am Grateful

Today, I am grateful for

Name:

Date:

Today, I am grateful for

Name:

Date:

Today, I am grateful for

Name:

Date:

Today, I am grateful for

Name:

Date:

I Am Grateful

Today, I am grateful for

Name:

Date:

Today, I am grateful for

Name:

Date:

Today, I am grateful for

Name:

Date:

Today, I am grateful for

Name:

Date:

I Am Grateful

Today, I am grateful for

Name:

Date:

Today, I am grateful for

Name:

Date:

Today, I am grateful for

Name:

Date:

Today, I am grateful for

Name:

Date:

I Am Grateful

Today, I am grateful for

Name:

Date:

Today, I am grateful for

Name:

Date:

Today, I am grateful for

Name:

Date:

Today, I am grateful for

Name:

Date:

I Am Grateful

Today, I am grateful for

Name:

Date:

Today, I am grateful for

Name:

Date:

Today, I am grateful for

Name:

Date:

Today, I am grateful for

Name:

Date:

Today, I am grateful for

Name:

Date:

Today, I am grateful for

Name:

Date:

Today, I am grateful for

Name:

Date:

Today, I am grateful for

Name:

Date:

I Am Grateful

Today, I am grateful for

Name:

Date:

Today, I am grateful for

Name:

Date:

Today, I am grateful for

Name:

Date:

Today, I am grateful for

Name:

Date:

I Am Grateful

Today, I am grateful for

Name:

Date:

Today, I am grateful for

Name:

Date:

Today, I am grateful for

Name:

Date:

Today, I am grateful for

Name:

Date:

I Am Grateful

Today, I am grateful for

Name:

Date:

Today, I am grateful for

Name:

Date:

Today, I am grateful for

Name:

Date:

Today, I am grateful for

Name:

Date:

I Am Grateful

Today, I am grateful for

Name:

Date:

Today, I am grateful for

Name:

Date:

Today, I am grateful for

Name:

Date:

Today, I am grateful for

Name:

Date:

I Am Grateful

Today, I am grateful for

Name:

Date:

Today, I am grateful for

Name:

Date:

Today, I am grateful for

Name:

Date:

Today, I am grateful for

Name:

Date:

I Am Grateful

Today, I am grateful for

Name:

Date:

Today, I am grateful for

Name:

Date:

Today, I am grateful for

Name:

Date:

Today, I am grateful for

Name:

Date:

I Am Grateful

Today, I am grateful for

Name:

Date:

Today, I am grateful for

Name:

Date:

Today, I am grateful for

Name:

Date:

Today, I am grateful for

Name:

Date:

I Am Grateful

Today, I am grateful for

Name:

Date:

Today, I am grateful for

Name:

Date:

Today, I am grateful for

Name:

Date:

Today, I am grateful for

Name:

Date:

I Am Grateful

Today, I am grateful for

Name:

Date:

Today, I am grateful for

Name:

Date:

Today, I am grateful for

Name:

Date:

Today, I am grateful for

Name:

Date:

I Am Grateful

Today, I am grateful for

Name:

Date:

Today, I am grateful for

Name:

Date:

Today, I am grateful for

Name:

Date:

Today, I am grateful for

Name:

Date:

I Am Grateful

Today, I am grateful for

Name:

Date:

Today, I am grateful for

Name:

Date:

Today, I am grateful for

Name:

Date:

Today, I am grateful for

Name:

Date:

I Am Grateful

Today, I am grateful for

Name:

Date:

Today, I am grateful for

Name:

Date:

Today, I am grateful for

Name:

Date:

Today, I am grateful for

Name:

Date:

I Am Grateful

Today, I am grateful for

Name:

Date:

Today, I am grateful for

Name:

Date:

Today, I am grateful for

Name:

Date:

Today, I am grateful for

Name:

Date:

I Am Grateful

Today, I am grateful for

Name:

Date:

Today, I am grateful for

Name:

Date:

Today, I am grateful for

Name:

Date:

Today, I am grateful for

Name:

Date:

I Am Grateful

Today, I am grateful for

Name:

Date:

Today, I am grateful for

Name:

Date:

Today, I am grateful for

Name:

Date:

Today, I am grateful for

Name:

Date:

I Am Grateful

Today, I am grateful for

Name:

Date:

Today, I am grateful for

Name:

Date:

Today, I am grateful for

Name:

Date:

Today, I am grateful for

Name:

Date:

Today, I am grateful for

Name:

Date:

Today, I am grateful for

Name:

Date:

Today, I am grateful for

Name:

Date:

Today, I am grateful for

Name:

Date:

Printed in Great Britain
by Amazon

36708371R00126